3 1943 00093 8138

NORTH RIVERSIDE PUBLIC LIBRARY

D0110749

9/06

WALT DISNEY'S
DONALD DUCK
ADVENTURES

TAKE-ALONG COMIC

GEMSTONE PUBLISHING
TIMONIUM, MARYLAND

NORTH RIVERSIDE PUBLIC LIBRARY

STEPHEN A. GEPPI
*President/Publisher and
Chief Executive Officer*

JOHN K. SNYDER JR.
Chief Administrative Officer

STAFF

LEONARD (JOHN) CLARK
Editor-in-Chief

GARY LEACH
Associate Editor

SUE KOLBERG
Assistant Editor

TRAVIS SEITLER
Art Director

SUSAN DAIGLE-LEACH
Production Associate

DAVID GERSTEIN
Archival Editor

MELISSA BOWERSOX
Director-Creative Projects

• IN THIS ISSUE •

Donald Duck
Where's the Bin Been? **†*
Story: Pat & Carol McGreal **Art:** Flemming Andersen

Mickey Mouse
The Wind of the Azalai
Story: Augusto Macchetto **Art:** Guiseppe Dalla Santa
Lettering: Sue Kolberg

The Beagle Boys
The Black Sheep †
Story: Francesco Artibani **Art:** Silvia Ziche

Donald Duck
Inside Donald Duck **†*
Story: Mark & Laura Shaw **Art:** Flemming Andersen

Original story color by **Egmont
Color modifications and †lettering by **Gary Leach***

ADVERTISING/ MARKETING

J.C. VAUGHN
Executive Editor

BRENDA BUSICK
Creative Director

JAMIE DAVID
Director of Marketing

SARA ORTT
Marketing Assistant

HEATHER WINTER
Office Manager
Toll Free
(888) 375-9800 Ext. 249
ads@gemstonepub.com

MARK HUESMAN
Production Assistant

MIKE WILBUR
Shipping Manager

RALPH TURNER
Accounting Manager

**ANGIE MEYER
JUDY GOODWIN**
Subscriptions
Toll Free (800) 322-7978

**WALT DISNEY'S
DONALD DUCK
ADVENTURES 19**
Take-Along Comic
July, 2006

Published by
Gemstone Publishing

© 2006 Disney Enterprises, Inc.,
except where noted.
All rights reserved.

Nothing contained herein may be
reproduced without the written
permission of Disney Enterprises,
Inc., Burbank, CA., or other
copyright holders. 12-issue
subscription rates: In the U.S.,
$95.40. In Canada, $105.00,
payable in U.S. funds. For advertising rates and information call
(888) 375-9800 ext. 413.
Subscription and advertising
rates subject to change without
notice. Postmaster: send address
changes to Walt Disney's Donald
Duck Adventures / Take-Along
Comic, PO Box 469, West Plains,
MO, 65775.

PRINTED IN CANADA

NORTH RIVERSIDE PUBLIC LIBRARY

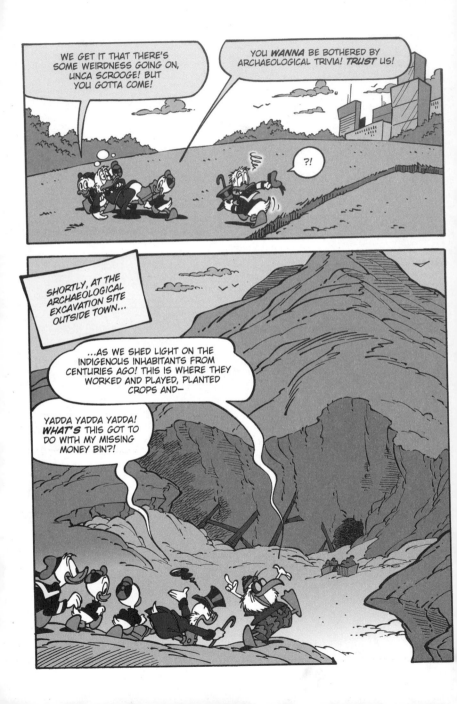

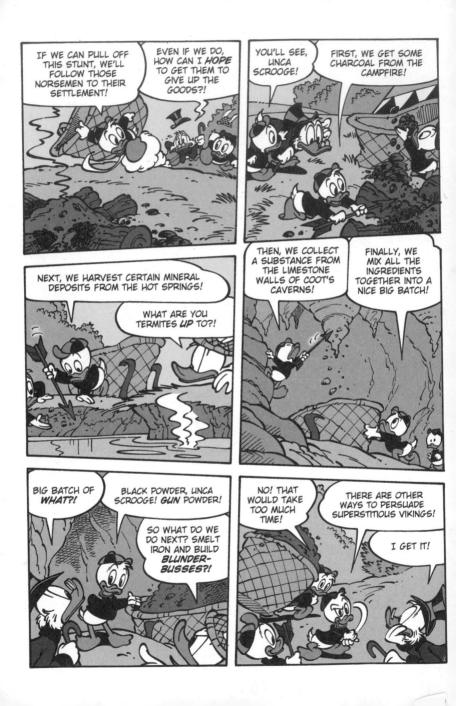

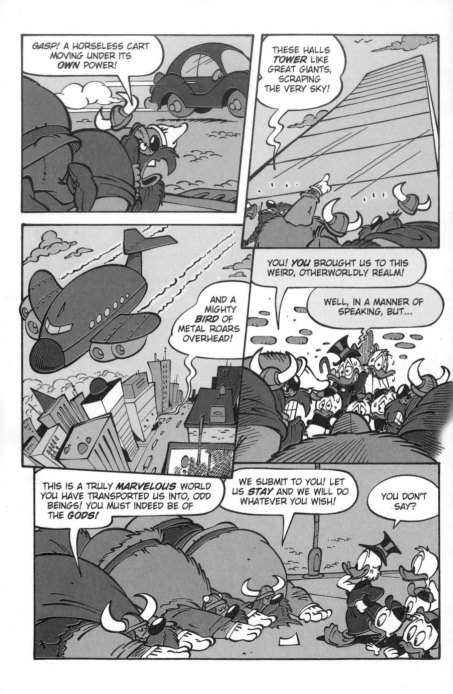

PRECISELY! WOULD YOU LIKE TO JOIN OUR EXPEDITION?

SURE! WE WERE GOING TO THE *OCEAN*, BUT WE CAN CHANGE OUR PLANS! ARE YOU WITH ME, GOOFY?

WHY NOT? AFTER ALL, THE SAHARA'S LIKE A BIG *BEACH* AND I'M ALREADY EQUIPPED! I'VE GOT A *DIVIN' MASK*, A LITTLE *BUCKET*, A *SHOVEL*...

OKAY, BUT THEY WON'T BE MUCH USE!

FINE! PROFESSOR MARLIN WILL TAKE CARE OF THE MUSEUM WHILE *BILL LEE*, OUR NEW ASSISTANT, WILL ACCOMPANY US! HE'S A WIZARD WITH NEW TECHNOLOGY LIKE *GPS**!

YOU'RE TOO KIND, PROFESSOR ZAPOTEC!

*GLOBAL POSITIONING SYSTEM, A LOCATION SYSTEM BASED ON SIGNALS TRANSMITTED BY A GROUP OF SATELLITES!

DON'T BE SO MODEST! YOUR RESUMÉ SHOWS THAT YOU ARE ALSO AN EXPERT ARCHAEOLOGIST, YOU SPEAK TWELVE LANGUAGES, YOU DANCE THE FLAMENCO...

...YOU'RE GOOD WITH A BOW AND ARROW, YOU PLAY THE OBOE... AND YOU'RE AN EXCELLENT COOK!

YUM!

PHOOEY! WHAT A *SHOW-OFF*!

IT'S TRUE! IN HIS BOOK, *HISTORY*, HERODOTUS* SPOKE OF THE SAHARA AS IF IT WERE A GARDEN!

SO IT WAS!

*ANCIENT GREEK HISTORIAN

"THE SAND HAD NOT YET CONQUERED, AND THE DESERT WAS NOT YET A... DESERT!"

THEN THE SUN AND THE WIND TRIUMPHED! THE WATER DRIED UP AND THE PLANTS BOWED THEIR LEAVES, DEFEATED FOREVER! TRAVEL BETWEEN THE TWO CITIES BECAME *DIFFICULT* AND *DANGEROUS...*

...UNTIL OUR ANCIENT FOREFATHERS, FOUND A WAY TO JOURNEY IN PERPETUAL *COOLNESS!* COME WITH ME!

BY THIS MEANS, WE CAN CONFOUND THE CURIOUS... AND JOURNEY UNSEEN AND IN SAFETY ON OUR *SHIPS OF THE DESERT!*

YOU MEAN *CAMELS!*

SOMETIMES... BUT ONLY IF WE ARE NOT IN A *HURRY!*

?

NOW FOLLOW ME! I WILL SHOW YOU YOUR NEW HOME!

BUT I DON'T GET IT... WHERE'D ALL THAT AIR COME FROM?

THE WIND IS CREATED WHEN THE ATMOSPHERIC PRESSURE IN TWO DISTANT PLACES IS DIFFERENT!

THE TWO CITIES ARE FAR ENOUGH APART TO CAUSE POWERFUL WINDS IN THE INTERIOR OF THE TUNNEL, WHICH THEY HAVE LEARNED HOW TO USE!

AT THAT MOMENT, IN GHEEMMA, THE WHITE CITY...

HUH? WHAT COULD BE HAPPENING? FIRST THE *ALARM*, AND NOW... *THIS!*

EVERYONE, COME QUICKLY! WE HAVE AN EMERGENCY!

KA-BOOMM...

OUR BROTHERS AND SISTERS IN AUHRATT HAVE *NEED* OF US!

WITH WHAT SHOULD I LOAD THE CANNON, SAPHORITT?

WHAT A QUESTION!

WITH *SALT!*

LET'S GO! WE MUST SAVE THE *ROAD OF SHADOW!*

NORTH RIVERSIDE PUBLIC LIBR

NORTH RIVERSIDE PUBLIC LIBRARY

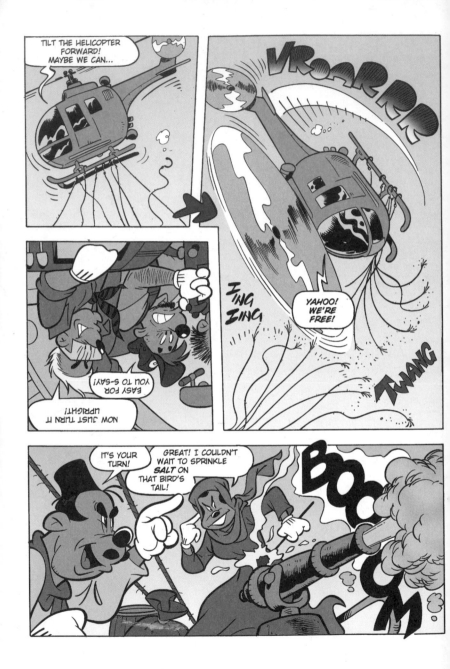

Subscribe!

Mail this coupon to: Gemstone Publishing, P.O. Box 469, West Plains, Missouri 65775.
MO residents add 6.975% sales tax; MD residents add 5% sales tax.

☐ Walt Disney's Comics and Stories: $83.40 for 12 issues   ☐ Walt Disney's Uncle Scrooge: $83.40 for 12 issues
   ($90.00 Canada, payable in US funds)   ($90.00 Canada, payable in US funds)
☐ Walt Disney's Donald Duck and Friends: $35.40 for 12 issues   ☐ Walt Disney's Mickey Mouse and Friends: $35.40 for 12 issues
   ($40.00 Canada, payable in US funds)   ($40.00 Canada, payable in US funds)
☐ D.D.A.: $95.40 for 12 issues ($105.00 Canada, payable in US funds)

Name: _____

Address: _____

City: _____ State: _____ Zip Code: _____

Email: _____

☐ Visa   ☐ MC   ☐ Other   Card #_____ Exp. Date: _____

GEMSTONE PUBLISHING

Yes, Mickey, Minnie, Donald, Uncle Scrooge and many other of your favorite Disney
characters can be delivered right to your doorstep every month when you subscribe to
Gemstone's exciting line of Disney comics. That means incredible convenience
and incredible fun for you!

Whether it's Walt Disney's Comics and Stories and Uncle Scrooge, providing the best
of vintage and recent classic tales by highly-acclaimed creators, or Donald Duck
Adventures, the 5" X 7½" "Take-Along Comic" series with exciting modern
stories, or even Donald Duck and Mickey Mouse and Friends, offering
Disney fans the best contemporary Mouse and Duck stories
in the familiar 32-page, stapled, comic book
format.

©2005 Disney
Enterprises, Inc.

SHIVER ME FROZEN TAILFEATHERS!

TWO FROSTY TALES FROM THE SNOWY BADLANDS OF THE YUKON!

GEMSTONE
PUBLISHING

$6.95

WALT DISNEY
presents

Donald Duck in SOMEWHERE in NOWHERE

Uncle $crooge in NORTH of the YUKON

© 2006 Disney Enterprises Inc.

Hop aboard a dogsled bound for adventure as your favorite Disney ducks, Donald and Uncle Scrooge, tangle with some cold-hearted Klondike crooks!

"Somewhere in Nowhere," a unique collaboration between Carl Barks, John Lustig, and Pat Block, marks the last duck adventure on which Barks worked! When Donald tries to get rich in Alaska, the money-making scheme leads to a race against time with the evil Hamalot McSwine!

Then, in Barks' 1965 classic "North of the Yukon," the race is between Scrooge and old-time rival Soapy Slick... with the stakes involving an IOU that could impound the McDuck millions!

Donald Duck and Uncle Scrooge—two feature-length duck epics in one $6.95, 64-page trade paperback. **Mush,** you huskies!

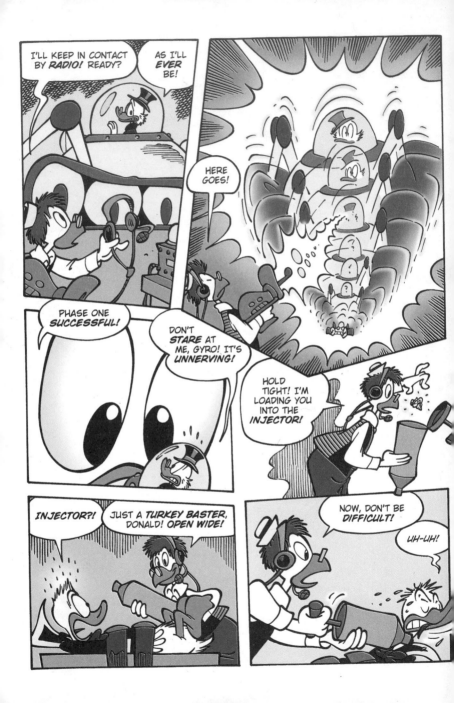

NORTH RIVERSIDE PUBLIC LIBRARY

GEMSTONE PUBLISHING PRESENTS

More DuckTales

before they were DuckTales by Carl Barks

VOLUME 2

ON SALE JULY 2006!

DISNEY PRESENTS CARL BARKS' GREATEST **DuckTales** STORIES VOLUME 2

We knew how much you would enjoy the works of Carl Barks in our first presentation of his *"duck tales before they were DuckTales,"* so we've assembled a second volume containing the remaining Barks stories that were adapted into *DuckTales* cartoons! Yes, more of your favorite duck characters along with an array of appearances by various villains.

Here's what you can expect:

- Relive Uncle Scrooge's Himalayan bottlecap adventure *"Tralla La"*

- Travel along with Scrooge as he searches for glittering wool in *"The Golden Fleecing"*

- Discover every kind of diamond imaginable (Carl Barks kind of imaginable) in *"The Status Seeker"*

- The Beagle Boys are at it again, this time taking on *"The Unsafe Safe"*

- What? Someone else after Scrooge's money in *"The Horseradish Story"*?

- *"Giant Robot Robbers"* run wild in Duckburg with one particular Money Bin in their sights!

Enjoy!

© 2006 Disney Enterprises Inc

GEMSTONE PUBLISHING

Need help finding a comic shop near you? Visit the Comic Shop Locator Service at http://csls.diamondcomics.com or call 1-888-COMIC-BOOK (toll-free)!

get a

DOUBLE DIP OF FUN!

It's FREE!

Every week Scoop - the free e-newsletter - serves up a heaping double dip of comic character twins. From Heckle and Jeckle to the Wonder Twins to Mary-Kate and Ashley Olsen. Just log onto http://scoop.diamondgalleries.com to subscribe. Scoop spoons up two times as much trendy, tasty tidbits as any other pop culture site. It's just dripping with news, collectible info, and fun facts!

SCOOP- IT'S INFORMA- LICIOUS . . . AND IT'S FAT-FREE!

All characters TM and © respective copyright holders. All rights reserved.

Gemstone Publishing presents

More Life and Times of SCROOGE MᶜDUCK

Walt Disney's
The Life and Times of
$CROOGE MᶜDUCK
Companion

by
DON ROSA

© 2006 Disney Enterprises, Inc.

You asked for them, and here they are... the prequels, the sequels, and the in-between-quels to Don Rosa's *Life and Times of Scrooge McDuck!* Filling in the gaps between the twelve original chapters are "The Cowboy Captain of the Cutty Sark" (Chapter 3B/*Uncle Scrooge* 318), "The Vigilante of Pizen Bluff" (Chapter 6B/*US* 306), "The Prisoner of White Agony Creek" (the all-new Chapter 8B!), "Hearts of the Yukon" (Chapter 8C/*Walt Disney Giant* 1) and "The Sharpie of the Culebra Cut" (Chapter 10B/*US* 332).

But wait... there's more! We've got Don's first look at Scrooge's youth—the famous flashback from "Last Sled to Dawson" (*Uncle Scrooge Adventures* 5). We've got the apocrypha: "Of Ducks and Dimes and Destinies" (Chapter 0/*US* 297) and "The Dream of a Lifetime!" (*US* 329), with the modern-day Magica De Spell and Beagle Boys wreaking havoc in Scrooge's past. And we've got the commentary—more than a dozen pages of Rosa recollections on how these classics came to be, all for only $16.99!

STILL ON SALE
(AT A TIGHTWAD-FRIENDLY PRICE!)

It's Rosa's original twelve-chapter quest into Scrooge's life—presented in a 264-page volume replete with extensive authorial commentary. From Scrooge's Scottish childhood to his worldwide quest for gold; from his ill-starred romances to his meetings with history's heroes, this classic biography marked a milestone in duck comics. Annotated by Rosa himself and full of new-to-North-America art, Gemstone's $16.99 collected edition belongs on every Disney fan's bookshelf.

Walt Disney's
The Life and Times of
SCROOGE MᶜDUCK

DON ROSA

© 2006 Disney Enterprises, Inc.

GEMSTONE
PUBLISHING